A PRESIDENT'S COUNTRY

LBJ receiving a copy of the first edition of A PRESIDENT'S COUNTRY from Jack Maguire

A PRESIDENT'S

A Guide to the LBJ Country of Texas

COUNTRY

Edited by JACK MAGUIRE

with drawings by MAC TATCHELL

SHOAL CREEK PUBLISHERS, INC.
P.O. Box 968
Austin, Texas 78767

Design and Typography by Kim Taylor

Photographs by Jim Seymour, Cader A. Shelby and Frank Wolfe

Printed in the U.S.A. by Steck-Warlick, Austin, Texas

CONTENTS

Hill Country deer

INTRODUCTION

HOW THIS BOOK CAME TO BE WRITTEN

This is the story, not of a man, but of the land he lived in and loved.

It is, like the man, marked by contrast.

It has been called a harsh land because, as Walter Prescott Webb said, it has been "burned by drought, beaten by hail, withered by hot winds, frozen by blizzards."

Yet it is a gentle land of little hills and verdant valleys, of limestone springs and forests of perennially green cedar and live oak.

It is, by geographical definition, a part of the nation's southland, yet it is western by culture and tradition. Texans know it as the "Hill Country." Since November 22, 1963, however, many of the hill folk have proudly renamed it "a President's country."

For more than 64 years, this narrow strip of real estate stretching through the heartland of Texas was both a home and a tranquilizer for Lyndon Baines Johnson, 36th President of the United States. Here he was born on August 27, 1908, in a simple frame house near the banks of his beloved Pedernales River. Here he built his famous LBJ Ranch, the beautiful retreat to which he escaped from the pressures of more than three

LBJ and Lady Bird at the ranch

decades of political life. And here, on January 22, 1973, he died.

Like the land which he came from, and which ultimately received him, Lyndon Johnson could be gentle and harsh, exuberant and brooding; his moods were subject to Texas-size fluctuations. It has been said that all men reflect their origins; in Lyndon Johnson, the rough terrain around the Pedernales left a lasting mark. Certainly it was the bleak, rugged and poignant Hill Country that shaped and molded him, relaxed and comforted him and, perhaps, gave him his place in history.

He always felt that to understand a man's strengths and weaknesses, one had to know something of the land that gave him birth, educated him and which was the place to which he returned to renew his soul. And so it was that he wanted all America to know the land of small ranches and smaller farms, of peach orchards and pastures, that always would be his personal Shangri-La. He wanted this so much, in fact, that he asked some of his friends to put the story together so others could know something more of his beloved Hill Country.

This book really began one day in 1940 when Lyndon Johnson and I met for the first time. I was a young reporter on the Denison (Texas) *Herald* when a tall, curly-haired man walked into the editorial office late one afternoon and announced: "My name is Lyndon Johnson and I'd like to buy somebody a cup of coffee."

I was the sole occupant of the office at that moment, so I walked with him a block down the street to a little cafe. There

3

I had my first (and, in some ways, my most memorable) visit with a man whose friendship I was to value for almost 33 years. Curiously, we had much to talk about that day, primarily because we talked most about a man we both admired—Sam Rayburn.

"Mr. Sam" had been my Congressman all of my life, and Congressman Johnson made it clear that Mr. Sam was not only his great friend, but also his mentor. He had, in fact, come to Denison that day for one purpose—to board the Katy Railroad's *Texas Special* because he knew that Mr. Sam would be taking the train back to Washington that afternoon. The young Congressman from the Tenth District wanted an uninterrupted two nights and a day on the Pullman to visit with the man who was to influence his own life so significantly.

It was two or three years before I saw Lyndon Johnson again. But I heard from him occasionally—a note, a telephone call, and in 1941, an autographed picture of Lieutenant Commander Johnson sent from MacArthur's Headquarters in the Pacific. That picture, along with an autographed Presidential portrait, still hangs on my office wall.

After my wife, Pat, and I moved to Austin in 1950, it seems that our lives and those of the Johnsons intertwined in myriad ways. I remember one Thanksgiving Day when our sons, Jack and Kevin, were young and Lynda Bird and Luci were not much older, the Senator called and asked that Pat and I come down to the LBJ Ranch for a talk. He insisted that we bring the boys, and he put them in the back seat of the car while he drove me over the ranch and tried to persuade me to join his staff in Washington. He never understood why I preferred the quiet life of Austin to the hectic and exciting political one that he was beginning to dominate in Washington.

There are so many memories, like the whirlwind trip I made with him to Hyannis Port in 1960 for his first meeting with Senator John F. Kennedy following the Democratic Convention that had nominated them for the presidency and vice-presidency. With a chartered Viscount loaded with staff and press, we left Austin early on a Friday morning, stopped off in Kansas City for lunch with former President Truman, set down in Cleveland for an airport visit with local Democratic leaders and arrived on Cape Cod in a driving rainstorm after midnight. The Kennedys (who had planned to meet us) had given up and gone home.

Before we returned to Austin on Sunday night, we had flown on to Nashville for a speech, then to Iowa for another. In three days, we had touched the Eastern seaboard, the Deep South and the Middle West. Lyndon Johnson liked that kind of pace. He moved with the speed of a Texas blue norther, sweeping everything and everybody along with him.

It was a pace that he never slackened during the campaign that fall. And on the following January 20, John F. Kennedy, the young sophisticate from Massachusetts, and Lyndon Johnson, the rancher from Texas, became the new President and Vice-President of the most powerful nation on earth.

My contacts with the new Vice-President were varied, if infrequent. Once when I was in Washington on business, he called me out of an important meeting to insist that Pat and I come to dinner at "The Elms." It turned out that he was concerned about some editorials that had been printed in *The Daily Texan*, the student newspaper at The University of Texas. I was convenient, and so we argued until almost midnight about whether or not Lynda Johnson should come to the University (from which her mother holds two degrees) or go to Southwest Texas State, which he had attended.

I was delighted when she eventually chose The University of Texas. So was he, I think.

The next time I saw Lyndon Johnson, he was President of the United States. It was on New Year's Eve, 1963, and it was then that the idea for this book was finally conceived.

The previous November 22, President Kennedy had been assassinated in downtown Dallas. Vice-President Johnson, who was riding in the same automobile caravan, had assumed the nation's highest office by taking the oath aboard Air Force One at Dallas' Love Field. He had returned to Washington almost immediately, flying aboard the presidential jet that bore the body of Mr. Kennedy back for a state funeral. The following few weeks were sad and busy ones for the new government, and it was not until the Christmas holidays that the President and Mrs. Johnson found time to come home to Texas for a little rest at the LBJ Ranch. I did not see him until New Year's Eve.

For some years, Pat and I have spent New Year's Eve with a number of other couples who are old friends. Traditionally we gather at somebody's house for a drink, then go to the country club dance. On this New Year's Eve, we were hosting the group and had invited some of our old friends on the White House staff who had accompanied the Johnsons to Texas to join us. These included Special Presidential Assistant Horace Busby and his wife, Mary Virginia; Liz Carpenter, Mrs. Johnson's press secretary; Bess Abel, social secretary at the White House, and Bill Moyers. About mid-afternoon, Busby called to say that the President would like to come also.

Mrs. Johnson decided to stay at the ranch, but the President came for cocktails. During the hour he was with us, he told me that he wanted to ask a special favor.

"I want you to put together something about the Hill Country of Texas," he said. "You can mimeograph it, or print it, or whatever, but get it done. I want to hand it out to the press—particularly the ones from the East. I want them to know and love this part of Texas as much as I do."

I didn't wait. The next day, I started calling people at The University of Texas to enlist their help. R. Henderson Shuffler, now director of the Institute of Texan Cultures in San Antonio, agreed to do a chapter on the history of the Hill Country. Dr. W.W. Newcomb, director of the University's Texas Memorial Museum and an authority on Indians, did two chapters—one on the Indians of the area, with the help of Curtis Tunnell, the Museum's curator of anthrolopology; the other on the flora and fauna, with an assist from Gerald Raun, the Museum's curator of zoology. Dr. Peter T. Flawn, a nationally-known economic geologist who was one of the party guests, took the assignment to dc the chapter on geology. Drury B. Alexander, an architect and an expert on the restoration of old buildings, was delighted to do the chapter on homes in the hills.

Later in the spring, the President and Mrs. Johnson came home again. By then, Pat and I had gathered and edited the manuscript, and we took it to the ranch for a final check by the Johnsons. The President read it that afternoon while we cruised on his boat over the beautiful lake at Kingsland and Mrs. Johnson read it later as we sat on the patio of the ranch house. Both made suggestions and penciled in corrections, but pronounced the manuscript ready for the printer.

From the time it was published in 1964 and throughout the Johnson years in the White House, *A President's Country* was always among the gifts that a visiting dignitary could expect to receive. President Johnson ordered several hundred copies bound in red leather and lettered in gold, and he delighted in autographing copies for important guests.

Once when my wife and I were attending a White House state dinner honoring the Right Honorable Harold Wilson, Prime Minister of Great Britain, the President presented a copy of the book to Mr. Wilson. Several years later, when the Prime Minister came to Austin to lecture at the Lyndon Baines Johnson School of Public Affairs, he told me over a drink that *A President's Country* was the first book that he had re-read in preparation for his Texas visit.

A President's Country was the principal topic of conversation the last time I saw President Johnson. It was New Year's Day, 1973—nine years and a day since we had first discussed the possibility of a book. We met at a private luncheon before the Cotton Bowl football classic in Dallas where we had both come to watch our favorite team, the University of Texas Longhorns, playing the Crimson Tide of the University of Alabama.

Football, however, was secondary on both of our agendas. He was anxious that a new edition of *A President's Country* be published and I promised him that I'd get to work on it immediately.

As we left the luncheon to go over to the stadium, he gave Pat a kiss and me a Johnson hug, and said: "Why don't you all drive down to the ranch someday and surprise us?"

"Mr. President," I replied, "if we came without an invitation, the Secret Service would arrest us."

"My friends can come and see me anytime they please," he said. "And you are my friends."

Less than a month later, Lyndon Baines Johnson was dead. But perhaps this new edition of a little book that was one of his favorites can serve as an invitation to all of his friends everywhere to come and visit "a President's country."

He would have liked that.

> *Jack Maguire*
> Austin, Texas
> April, 1973

HERE HISTORY WAS ONLY YESTERDAY

R. HENDERSON SHUFFLER
Director, Institute of Texan Cultures
at San Antonio

IN "A PRESIDENT'S COUNTRY" YOU ARE SO CLOSE TO HISTORY you can feel it.

Less than a long lifetime ago, this was a raw frontier, where settlers fought off marauding Indians and predatory animals to protect their isolated homesteads, where herds were gathered for drives up the trail to Kansas, and where the stagecoach was the principal public conveyance in broad expanses innocent of railroads.

In Austin, with its universities, laboratories and modern industries, or in the clean prosperous little towns of the Hill Country, it is hard to realize that the changes we call the advance of civilization have come so swiftly. Yet, the official records tell of an Indian raid in this area as late as 1875. The first railroad reached Austin in 1871; none penetrated the Hill Country to the west until well after the turn of the century. Cattle went "up the trail" to the northern markets as late as 1900.

Events which seem to belong only in history books have been real experiences in the everyday lives and family traditions of many people you will meet here. President Johnson, for example, delighted in showing visitors to his LBJ Ranch two stone forts with double-thick walls, each with twin slits at the sides for rifle fire. They were built by his grandfather, Samuel Ealy Johnson, less than 100 years ago, to protect the first settlers of that vicinity from frequent Indian raids.

Austin's Municipal Auditorium

The President also enjoyed telling visitors of how his grandmother, caught by a surprise Indian raid, saved her life by hiding in a tiny basement cellar.

Eliza Johnson's Ordeal

It happened in late July of 1869. The whole countryside was shocked by the brutal killing and scalping of the Thomas C. Felps family on Cypress Creek, a few miles north of what is now known as Johnson City. Young Tom Felps was shot and stabbed to death by the Comanches and his 19-year-old wife was beaten about the face and head with a war club, then speared through the breast. For some reason, the Indians took the woman's scalp but not her husband's. When the stripped and battered bodies were found, on July 22nd, the word went out for all the men of the area to gather and give chase to the savages.

One near neighbor was Samuel Ealy Johnson. Sam and his brother, Tom, had been raising cattle in the Texas Hill Country and driving them up the trail to the Kansas markets since the middle 1850's. Even with time out for service with the Confederate forces in the Civil War, they had built up considerable holdings in land and cattle.

When Sam Johnson joined his brother and the other men of the settlement in pursuit of the Indian war party, he left

Eroded Buda limestone, Austin

behind, in the little log cabin which was their home, his bride of two years and their baby. Black-haired, sharp-eyed Eliza Bunton Johnson wasn't the scary type. She was accustomed to being left alone, while her husband and his brother went off on cattle drives that lasted several months. Daughter of a frontiersman on the upper Colorado, she was the niece of John Wheeler Bunton, a signer of the Texas Declaration of Independence, who had fought as a footsoldier in the battle of San Jacinto.

Eliza Johnson was frightened, but not unnerved, when, as she was returning from the spring with a bucket of water, she saw Indians riding toward her house. The Comanches had evaded their pursuers and doubled back to raid the unprotected little settlement. She ran to the house, keeping out of sight. Grabbing up her baby and an extra diaper, she slipped down a short flight of steps into the basement storage cellar. As she closed the trap door over her head, she inched a braided rug over it as camouflage. Then she bound the extra diaper over the baby's mouth to prevent the infant's crying from giving away their hiding place.

As she crouched in the dark, cramped cellar, she heard the Indians enter the house and stomp across the floor over her head. They ransacked the place, while she wept silently at the wanton destruction of the beloved wedding presents she had brought so far by wagon. Then they left, going to the barn

Edwards limestone, Oak Hill

to look for horses. Fearful that the savages might return, or another war party might come along, Mrs. Johnson and her baby stayed in their hideaway until late that night, when Sam Johnson returned.

Ties to the Frontier

The harrowing experience of Mrs. Samuel Ealy Johnson was not unique. Many families in this area have equally close and memorable ties with the frontier. The Indian was undisputed master of this land less than a century and a quarter ago. He relinquished his claim only after a bitter and bloody fight which went on, sporadically, for almost 40 years.

Nor have his footprints disappeared. Even today it is a comparatively easy matter for a sharp-eyed novice to pick up flint arrowheads, knives and other artifacts left behind by the recently departed Red Man on the rocky hillsides and along the clear-running streams. These Indian relics are so commonplace that many an old ranch home displays a sizeable collection over the parlor mantel. One Austin hamburger chain even uses them as wall decorations in its neon-lit emporiums.

The Historic Half-Truth

It is true that this part of our country is less than four score years and ten from the harsh and hazardous days of the frontier. Yet this is only a part of the truth. It is also true

12

Limestone dike, Dripping Springs

that in less than half the time required to turn the older frontiers of the Midwest and East into civilized lands, this area has bridged the gap to modernity. If you expect to find the streets crowded with swaggering gunmen or the hilltowns peopled with country bumpkins, you are due for something of a shock.

The simple truth is that the frontier here never was quite the life of "nauseating loneliness" which some historians have pictured. Nor were the frontiersmen all uncouth hell-for-leather gun-toters who were totally unfamiliar with the niceties of life. Texas then, as now, attracted hordes of adventurous newcomers from all over the world. They came then, as they are coming now, simply because the new land offered a better opportunity than the one from which they came. Some were well-educated, well-to-do and had already attained status in their old surroundings; others came in the hope of acquiring these attributes.

Sophistication on the Frontier

In the lovely valley village of Sisterdale in the 1840's, the learned German villagers conversed solely in Latin at the weekly meetings of their scientific and philosophical society — while friendly Indians stood in the doorway of the meetinghouse and gaped. At Bettina, above Fredericksburg, in the same period, an astounding collection of professional men

Patton Store, Oak Hill (Now the Fortress Restaurant)

and artists attempted to establish an Utopia on communal principles. The bubble burst, but the talented colonists spread throughout the area.

Nor was there a lack of sophistication in circles outside these villages. The people of Austin were not abashed by the noble titles of Prince Solms and Baron Meusebach of the German colonies. They had long ago become accustomed to associating with Count Jean Peter Isidore Alphonse de Saligny, French *charge d'affaires* to the Texas Republic, whose house adorned a hill just east of town. For that matter, many of them, like Mirabeau Buonaparte Lamar and Sam Houston, had moved in elite circles long before they came to Texas. Lamar had been secretary to the Governor of Georgia, a leading newspaperman and recognized painter and poet. Houston had been Governor of Tennessee and a member of the United States Congress. These were in the earliest days.

Later came such men as Joseph Brodbeck, the Wurttemberg scholar who conducted school at Fredericksburg and, in his spare time, worked on plans for a flying machine. In 1865, nearly 40 years before the Wright brothers, he built and flew an airplane powered by a giant coil spring. It soared to treetop height with this unique power, then crashed. But, it did fly, and Brodbeck was one of the unsung heroes of aviation in the days before the invention of the internal combustion engine.

14

Building date marker, Oak Hill

Old World Culture in the New

What better example of worldliness could you find than Louis von Hagen, late Captain of the Prussian army, who taught at Fredericksburg in the 1870's, and at the celebration of the town's 25th anniversary called the square dances at the Bismarck Garten — in French? Or Sir Swante Palm, the erudite political refugee from Sweden, who came to Austin in 1850 and became a merchant and officeholder, devoting much of his time to his true love of collecting fine books? The gift of his library to the fledgling University of Texas in 1897 more than doubled the university's book collection and set it on the way to becoming one of the great libraries of the nation. Palm's nephew, Swen Magnus Swenson, proved to be a financial genius. He built his little Austin enterprise into a fortune which made him one of the dominant figures in New York financial circles of the '90's.

Emir Hamvasy, exiled former Lord Mayor of Budapest, was professor of music at Swancoat's Academy in Austin in the late 1860's, until he abandoned music for the ministry. George Bonnell, newspaperman-politician, gave Austin its start toward becoming the literary and publishing center of this part of the world by writing and publishing the first book here in 1840, only a year after the town was laid out.

In the years which followed, in the ferment of an exciting, growing area, other names cropped up which are now known

Old stone structure, Dripping Springs

nationally and internationally. There was Elisabet Ney, noted Westphalian sculptress, who had done statues of King Ludwig II, Bismarck and Schopenhauer before she came to Austin and immortalized in marble such Texans as Sam Houston, Stephen Austin and Albert Sidney Johnston.

Men of Letters

Knox and Sweet moved their little Austin magazine, "Texas Siftings," to New York in 1884, and became among the first successful publishers of a national humor magazine. William Cowper Brann in 1891 started here his vitriolic commentary, "The Iconoclast," which in a few years became the most-read journal in America. And a good-natured ne'er-do-well drug store, land office and bank clerk named William Sidney Porter watched these successes and dreamed of the day when he would have the time to write. When he found the time, in a jail cell later, he emerged as a national figure called O. Henry.

Since then the names of such writers of this region as J. Frank Dobie, Walter Prescott Webb and Roy Bedichek have become familiar to all literate Americans. The University of Texas Press is nationally recognized as one of the great university publishing houses of the country and the literary collections of The University, in rare books, documents and manuscripts, are the envy of great centers of learning throughout the world.

16

Field on clay, Dripping Springs

Early Explorations

In contrast with its brief history of peaceful settlement by people of European stock, the country has a comparatively long record of penetration and temporary occupation by civilized groups. The first serious exploration of the region was made in the summer of 1691 by Domingo Teran de los Rios, newly appointed governor of "the province of the Tejas and adjacent regions."

The Spanish crown had directed Teran to blaze a new, more direct road from the provincial capital to Monclova (Mexico) to the missions established a few years earlier among the Tejas Indians, on the Louisiana border. He made his way up from Monclova, through the present site of San Antonio, to find a crossing of the Guadalupe River near where the town of San Marcos now stands. Fords which could be used the year around by heavily-laden packmules and clumsy Mexican carts were necessary anchorpoints of any usable road. From ford to ford, Teran and his party blazed their trail, which was to become *El Camino Real* (the King's Highway), the greatest thoroughfare across Texas for a century and a half.

From the Guadalupe ford, they ranged north and east, toward the Colorado. Passing through the rolling country southeast of present Austin, they found their next crossing at

Stair-step topography, Henly

the point where the town of Bastrop is now located. El Camino Real soon was extended to Natchitoches, to connect the Spanish of Mexico with the French of Louisiana. It brought to the Hill Country many of the early travelers and some of the earliest attempts at settlement.

Missions on the Colorado

The Franciscan fathers plodded along this wilderness trail throughout the 18th century to visit their ill-starred missions in East Texas. They finally abandoned the East Texas venture under pressure of the French and a growing hostility from the Indians. They then packed their limited supplies and trudged back along El Camino Real to establish three missions near the present site of Austin. A monument in Austin's Zilker Park, on a rise above the famed Barton Springs, marks the approximate location.

The Missions of San Jose de los Nazonis, San Francisco de los Neches and Nuestra Senora de la Purisima Concepcion de los Hainai, as they were called, lasted only one year in the wilderness along the Colorado. In 1731 they were removed to their present sites in the San Antonio area. There soldiers of the presidio could give them better protection from the hostile Indians and supplies could be more readily secured. These ancient missions are today among the showplaces of San Antonio.

Stair-step topography, Hays-Blanco County line

San Marcos de Neve

Three-quarters of a century after the failure of the missions on the Colorado, the King of Spain decided to create an outpost of civilization in this hostile land. He commissioned a wealthy soldier-politician, Don Felipe Roque de la Portilla, to establish a townsite on the bluff above the Guadalupe River at the Camino Real crossing. The Villa de San Marcos de Neve was laid out in 1807, and Don Felipe moved in with his herds, herdsmen and a half dozen families.

The Indians of the area were warlike and hostile in the 1800's. The great distances across unpopulated lands to the centers of civilization created problems of supply. Internal political troubles in Mexico prevented the crown from sending reinforcements to protect the villagers. In four years the original town died and was abandoned. But it left its mark on the land. It was in the town of San Marcos, near this ancient site, that Lyndon Baines Johnson was to receive his education at Southwest Texas State University, some 120 years later.

Don Felipe gathered up as many of his cattle as he could for the long trek back to Mexico, but many of the animals were left to fend for themselves. When the first Anglo settlers pushed up the Colorado from Stephen Austin's colony on the lower river, in the late 1820's, they found remnants of Don Felipe's cattle running wild with the buffalo. The cows, they reported, were even wilder than the bison, and only the

19

Hill Country, Blanco County

canniest hunter could get close enough to shoot one.

Jake Harrell's Stockade

One of these hunters was Jacob M. Harrell, who finally pitched his tent and settled down in 1835. A year or so later Jake Harrell built a little log cabin and enclosed it with a rail stockade. This was on the north bank of the river, near a ford, at the point where Shoal Creek flows into the Colorado. (*The starting point of the road map which is found in this booklet, the southwest corner of the Austin Municipal Auditorium, is almost directly across the river from the spot on which this first permanent habitation in the Austin area was erected. Looking north from the starting point, you can see the little bridge across Shoal Creek, where it flows into the Colorado. Near the east end of the bridge is the site of Harrell's cabin.*)

Soon other settlers gathered around, using the stockade as a haven when Indians attacked. A mile or more to the southwest, the grizzled old frontiersman, William Barton, made his home above the springs, near where the old Spanish missions had stood.

"The Daniel Boone of Texas"

William Barton, or "Uncle Billy," as he was known to the settlers, was an exceptionally rugged individualist, even for

Fossil clams on limestone　　　　　Madrone tree, Miller Creek

that day. A South Carolinian who had fought in the Indian wars in Alabama, he had come to Texas before 1830. When the nearest neighbors were within ten miles of his cabin in the LaGrange area, he had complained that the country was getting too crowded, and moved on up the Colorado. He settled at what we now call Barton Springs soon after Jake Harrell located at what is now Austin.

Seat of Future Empire

In the fall of 1838, the dashing Mirabeau Buonaparte Lamar, President-elect of the Republic of Texas, visited this area on a buffalo hunt. He was reportedly accompanied by his secretary — Edward Fontaine, great-grandson of Patrick Henry — and a small group of rangers from nearby Fort Prairie. The party slept their first night in Jake Harrell's stockade, and next morning ranged the countryside which is now occupied by the city of Austin, killing buffalo.

According to Fontaine, they had killed all of the buffalo they wanted by mid-morning, and the hunting party gathered to rest on the hill now occupied by the Texas Capitol. As he looked over the country from this vantage point, viewing the rich rolling prairies caught in the bend of the Colorado, with the rugged wooded hills to the south and west, Lamar is reported to have exclaimed:

Old stone fence, Miller Creek

"This should be the seat of future empire!"

A few months later, when Congress named a commission to recommend a new site for the permanent capital of Texas, Lamar is said to have instructed them to take a long hard look at the area around Waterloo, the village which had grown up around Jake Harrell's stockade.

There was an intense rivalry between a number of Texas towns for location of the capital, but the commission selected Waterloo and renamed it in honor of Stephen Fuller Austin, the "father of Texas."

Indian Troubles Begin

With the capital established in an outpost on the edge of their territory, the Indians, who had been pushed up the Brazos and Colorado by the oncoming tide of settlers, gave ground slowly. They retreated into the hills to the south and west, and up the river valleys to the north. On the nights of the full moon they raided isolated settlers' cabins and even ventured into Austin itself.

The rugged Hill Country was their refuge. They lived along the clear streams in the wooded valleys, venturing out to raid the white settlements, and ambushing any who were hardy enough to follow them into the hills.

Austin might well have remained a precarious outpost on the edge of the Indian-occupied Hill Country for several

Close view of old stone fence, Miller Creek

decades. That it did not was the result of a combination of seemingly unrelated events in far-away lands and an amazing amount of skullduggery in Texas.

The Mainzer Aldesverein

The French revolution of July, 1830, which overthrew Charles X, shook the thrones of the petty German princes and threatened the whole fabric of absolutism throughout Central Europe. In reaction, the German rulers turned their country into a police state, severely oppressing all who showed any leaning toward liberalism. This set many men of intellect and energy to looking for a new land in which they might enjoy political freedom.

At the same time, Germany was suffering from its age-old problem of a heavy population on too little land. Many eager, hard-working farmers were without hope of ever owning farms, and many competent mechanics were without jobs. All of these people were exposed during this period to a series of alleged travel books, written by highly imaginative German authors, who described the newly-opened country of Texas as a veritable paradise.

A group of idealistic noblemen formed an organization called the *Mainzer Aldesverein*, with the dream of acquiring vast lands in Texas and establishing a German colony there. They hoped eventually, not only to enrich themselves with

19th century cabin, Hwy. 290

profitable new estates, but also to develop in the new world a strong German state, loyal to the mother country.

The impractical aristocrats were first ensnared by a French adventurer named Bourgeois who operated under the fictitious title of Chevalier Bourgeois d'Orvanne. He defrauded the Germans by selling them a grant in the San Antonio area which had actually expired several months earlier.

Next, a fast-talking Teutonic promoter, who had been in Texas as German consul, sold them an interest in a land contract involving vast unexplored West Texas acreages in the heart of hostile Indian country. Without investigating their purchases, the noblemen began shipping out boatloads of eager emigrants. Their fate, upon landing in Texas, unprepared and misinformed, was tragic.

In order to avert complete disaster, Prince Carl of Solms-Braunfels, who represented the *Aldesverein* as commissioner-general, bought 1300 acres of land on the Comal and Guadalupe rivers and settled many early immigrants there. This settlement, 50 miles southwest of Austin, was named New Braunfels, after Prince Solms' family castle in Germany.

Founding of Fredericksburg

Soon after this settlement was established, the improvident prince returned to Germany, to be succeeded by a practical, determined leader, Baron Ottfried, Hans von Meusebach.

German house, Miller Creek

Knowing that thousands more Germans were on their way to Texas, Meusebach set out with a small exploring party to seek new lands for them. In the heart of the Indian-infested Hill Country, some 75 miles northwest of New Braunfels, he bought 10,000 acres of good land, well-watered and timbered. The whole tract was laid out in 10-acre plots and distributed among the immigrants of 1845 and 1846. This was the beginning of Fredericksburg, at the western end of "a President's country."

The first years of the new settlement were unbelievably hard. The *Aldesverein* provided practically none of the funds it had promised for transportation and establishment of the immigrants after they reached Texas. Many were forced to walk from the coast to the settlements in the hills. The bones of hundreds who died along the way marked the route. Drouth and disease plagued the villages and dissatisfaction brought political turmoil.

Still, the stouthearted Meusebach held them together. He made peace with the Indians, who admired his courage and his flaming red beard and gave him the title of *El Sol Colorado*. "The Red Sun" led a small party of Germans into the very heart of Comanche country, on the San Saba River, in early 1847, and made a treaty with the head chiefs, which enabled his people to spread unmolested into the new western lands.

Another claim on the President

With Fredericksburg soon grown into a town of more than a thousand, and the Indians generally pacified, the country between this point and the capital at Austin began to fill up. By the 1850's many non-Germanic ranchers, like the Johnson brothers, were running cattle in the hills and a number of Anglo settlements sprang up at scattered points along the streams.

A World of Its Own

But even then the Texas Hill Country remained isolated, geographically and socially, a little world of its own with a strange Old World flavor. There were no railroads through the area until after 1917, and then very few. Although the main highway from San Antonio to the West passed through Fredericksburg after the gold rush of '49, it carried little but the travel of military men to and from the forts that were inching steadily westward along the frontier.

The cattle raised in the hills were trailed out once or twice a year to the Kansas markets. Cotton was hauled by wagon to San Antonio. Otherwise, the thrifty German villages were self-contained and self-sustaining. The settlers built sturdy homes of the native rock, cultivated their fields and orchards intensively in the way they had known in Germany, made their own furniture, clothes and shoes, all of the necessities and the few comforts they enjoyed.

President's boyhood home, Johnson City

Anti-Slavery Sentiment

Life here was very different from what it was in the rest of Texas and attitudes were as foreign as the language spoken on the village streets. The first Texas colonists had been largely from the Southern states, with plantation backgrounds and traditionally accustomed to the use of slaves. The Germans, as a whole, neither needed nor wanted slaves, and few could have afforded them if they had.

While the majority of Texans in the thickly settled river bottoms of East Texas raised cotton and sugar cane, the Germans of the Hill Country tended orchards and gardens, kept dairy stock and eventually brought in sheep and goats. One element of the German population was made up of thrifty hard-working small farmers and mechanics who substituted their own toil for that of slaves and pocketed the savings. The other group was made of highly educated patricians and professional folk, whose idealism and liberalism automatically made them opposed to slavery.

Civil War Troubles

When the Civil War came, the Hill Country counties voted overwhelmingly against secession and the German element generally refused to have anything to do with the Confederacy. Many young men from the area escaped through Mexico to join the federal forces, while some who stayed at home

Broken-slope roof farmhouse, Johnson City

worked secretly for the Union. As a result, during this period, the Germans were distrusted and abused by many hotheads.

One group of renegades, calling themselves the *Haengebund* or "Hanging Band," roamed the Hill Country, stringing up the helpless German farmers and confiscating their property in the name of the Confederacy. Much of the confiscated goods found its way into the black markets of San Antonio, sold for the personal benefit of the looters. The non-German people of the Hill Country, while strongly partisan for the Confederacy, also resented this abuse of their neighbors.

After the Civil War, with the abolition of slavery, the chief causes for friction between the Germans and their neighbors were removed and slowly the old enmities and distrusts disappeared. The thrifty, hard-working people of the hill area won the respect of their neighbors and the beauty of their clean quaint towns attracted many visitors. Today, the Texas Hill Country, with its clear, cold streams, its lovely wooded mountains and its delightful climate, is one of the choice summer vacation spots in Texas.

Lore and Legends

Among the appeals to vacationers are the lore and legends of this long-isolated land.

When Baron Meusebach led his men into the San Saba country in 1847 to make peace with the Comanches, he left

Blanco County Courthouse, Johnson City

the settlement unprotected. Indian lookouts along his route of march built huge fires on the mountaintops to signal to the chiefs back in their own camping grounds reports of his progress and of the number of troops he had with him.

The story is told that the German children in one lonely cabin near Fredericksburg were frightened by the Indian signal fires and ran to their mother to ask what they might mean. The courageous woman did not want to terrify her children by talking about the Indians. Instead, she recalled an old German myth of fairies burning dead wood in the spring to make way for new growth.

There had been no time for her children to learn about fairies on the raw frontier, so she substituted more familiar terms and told her youngsters that the rabbits had gathered wild flowers from the hillsides to bring to the Easter rabbit, who had built great fires on the hills under the cauldrons in which he cooked the Easter eggs, coloring them with the wild flowers.

The children loved the story. When the men returned from the Indian country, rejoicing over their peace treaty, they were told the tale. They vowed then that as long as the treaty held they would build fires on the hilltops around town each Easter eve. And so they have, for well over a hundred years.

The Fredericksburg Easter festival has grown into one of the most delightful observances of this special holiday in all

Blanco County Jail, Johnson City

the world. A pageant is held at the fairgrounds on Easter eve, which combines history, childhood fantasy and religious symbolism. Children gather wildflowers to fashion Easter nests, Indians parade across the fairgrounds, the colonists are depicted in their settlement of Fredericksburg, the famous peace treaty scene is re-enacted, and so is the story of the mother in her lonely cabin, telling her children the first version of this unique Easter story. The ceremony ends with religious observances and song, after which the fires flare high on the hilltops and the townspeople go quietly to their homes.

Enchanted Rock

In addition to its famous Bear Mountain, a massive mound of solid granite from which building materials have been quarried for many years, and the spectacular Balanced Rock, a huge boulder perched precariously on tiny spikes atop a nearby peak, the Fredericksburg area boasts a legendary natural site of unusual mystery and beauty. This is the Enchanted Rock, in the northeastern part of the country. A bald, oval granite mountain, it covers some 640 acres and towers a thousand feet above the surrounding hills. At its very top there is a group of grotesque stone figures, carved by wind and rain, surrounding a natural rock basin which holds a pool of water.

The Indians feared this mountain and avoided it. They thought the grotesque rock figures at its top were evil spirits.

Stone farm building, Johnson City

Their superstitions were enhanced by noises which came from the mountain at night, when the mass of rock cracked and creaked as it contracted while cooling off after the heat of the day.

Many legends have grown up around Enchanted Rock. The most popular tells of an Indian chief who took his only daughter to the top of the mountain and sacrificed her to his gods. Instead of being appeased, the gods were angered, and doomed him to wander forever on the mountaintop, bewailing his deed. From the summit of this mountain, in the fall of 1841, the famous ranger captain, Jack Hays, held out single-handed against a Comanche attack, inflicting such a heavy loss on the Indians that they finally fled. A lovely park, with a fine spring, at the base of the mountain is a favorite picnic spot.

Today's Hill Country

The country in which the 36th President of the United States grew up and to which he returned at every opportunity is no longer a quiet backwater, isolated by its hills from the mainstream of progress. Good roads and modern transportation have ended that era.

Today the people of the Hill Country get out to visit the cities, to attend the great universities, to tour this country and many others. And people from everywhere come into the

Stone barns, Johnson City

hills, as tourists and vacationers and to make their homes. The influx of "outlanders" which started with the establishment of summer homes in the hills by city folk eager to "get away from it all," has continued in an ever-increasing number of people who are building homes in the hills for their retirement.

Every hamlet in the area now boasts an excellent public library. Two of the best-known colonies of artists and writers in Texas are located at nearby Wimberley and Hunt.

The prosperity of the region, once you leave Austin, depends primarily on the products of the land — cattle, sheep and goats, poultry, peaches and wheat. A good and growing source of revenue is from hunters who flock into the hills each year and pay well for the privilege of harvesting the plentiful deer and wild turkeys.

Austin itself has grown from the few cabins clustered near Jake Harrell's stockade in 1838 to a modern city of around a quarter of a million people. Its principal activities center on politics — as the county seat and state capital — and education.

The University of Texas, with more than 40,000 students, is one of the top-ranking academic institutions of the nation. St. Edwards University, Huston-Tillotson College, Lutheran Concordia College, Austin Presbyterian Theological Seminary, The Episcopal Theological Seminary of the Southwest, as well as the State Schools for the Blind and the Deaf, add to its

Cambrian Age dolomite, Rocky Creek

importance as an educational center. The surrounding hills, valleys, spring-fed streams and lakes have made Austin a recreational center and in recent years location of electronic and other research-centered industries has contributed to its rapid growth.

THE REAL OLD-TIMERS WERE RED MEN

W. W. NEWCOMB, *Director*
and CURTIS TUNNELL, *Curator of Anthropology*
The Texas Memorial Museum
The University of Texas

FOR MORE THAN 12,000 YEARS, THE AREA BETWEEN AUSTIN AND Fredericksburg was Indian country.

The Texas Hill Country — "a President's country" — is rich in unrecorded history. When man first came to the Pedernales River Valley, perhaps even earlier than 12,000 years ago, he was the hunter of the large game animals prevalent in these late Pleistocene times. These Paleo-Indians used distinctively fluted and parallel-flaked spear points to bring down their quarry — the mammoths, mastodons, giant bison, horses and other animals common to the area. Even today their projectile points are scattered along the hillsides and major watercourses of the region.

Marks of the Archaic Cultures

By the time the last of the great ice-age animals had disappeared, about 8,000 years ago, new peoples had come to occupy the Hill Country. These, too, were hunters, but they also were gatherers of many wild plant foods. These Archaic cultures — and there appear to be many of them spaced over many millenia — left "a President's Country" a unique heritage. These are the strange burned rock middens, found near sources of water only in the Edwards Plateau region.

A midden, to a modern housewife, is simply an accumulation of refuse about a dwelling. These Indian middens, however, are king-size garbage heaps as much as an acre in

Old cotton gin, Hye

extent and eight feet thick. They are accretions of burned hearthstones mixed with dark soil, charcoal, stone tools, animal bones and mussel shells.

Limestone boulders were used by these early peoples as hearthstones, but they soon cracked and broke from the heat of cooking fires and new hearthstones had to be dragged into place. This process, repeated generation after generation, plus the accumulation of refuse incidental to the lives of many people, resulted in the construction of the middens.

Advent of the Bow and Arrow

About 500 A. D., other peoples and new ways of doing things came to the valley of the Pedernales. These Indians used the bow and arrow instead of the Archaic atlatl, or spear thrower, and tiny points (often called "bird points") replaced the larger dart points of Archaic times. These new peoples also made or traded for pottery vessels, but in other respects, they appear to have lived much as did their Archaic forerunners, hunting deer, bison, and other animals, gathering many seeds, tubers, nuts, and fruit. They frequently camped on the burned rock middens of their predecessors, in turn adding refuse to them. These people appear to have been ancestors of the Tonkawas, the Indians who occupied central Texas when it first became known to Europeans.

"Gingerbread" on Hye Post Office   Eroded limestone bluff

Tragedy of the Tonkawas

The earliest Spanish expeditions did not explore this area of Texas; nevertheless, the Tonkawas were soon adversely affected by their presence in this part of the world. Diseases to which the natives had little resistance, Spanish slave raids, and greatly increased strife with other Indian peoples served to reduce their strength. By the eighteenth century, when the Spanish attempted to consolidate their hold on Texas by establishing presidios and missions in central Texas, the Tonkawas were much weakened.

Originally there were a number of independent Tonkawa bands— the Mayeye, Yojaune, Ervipiame, Cavas, Emet, Sana, Toho, and Tohaha. Each band had a chief, and in time of war they also appear to have had special war leaders. The Tonkawas were bison hunters who also made much use of deer and smaller game, as well as many plant foods. The only mammals they did not consume, because of religious taboos, were wolves and their coyote kin. The Tonkawas are often recalled as cannibalistic, and it is true that they, as well as a number of other Texas Indians, sometimes ate parts of their enemies' bodies, but because of magical and religious convictions, not for hunger's sake.

Our Lipan Allies

In the early years of the eighteenth century, mounted Lipan

Turn-off to LBJ Ranch

and Mescalero Apaches arrived from the north and west to supplant the Tonkawas and to contend with the Spaniards for control of Central Texas. Before the coming of Europeans, their ancestors had occupied much of the southern plains, their more permanent settlements being located in river valleys where they grew some crops of corn, beans and squash. But their main food source was the huge bison which they followed over the tremendous expanses of the plains.

Horses, which these Apaches acquired from the Spanish and mastered in the seventeenth century, did much to increase the ease and efficiency with which bison could be hunted. But horses also made a bison-hunting existence more attractive to other tribes, and the subsequent history of the southern plains is one of bitter strife between competing tribes.

The Lipans, more closely associated with the Hill Country in the eighteenth century than the Mescaleros, were divided into a number of shifting, autonomous bands, each made up of several hundred people. They were a tribe only in the sense that they were a distinct cultural body—an unorganized group of bands sharing a common way of life.

The nomadic Lipan, like other Plains Indians, lived in bisonhide tipis, transported their possessions by use of a travois (a wooden frame dragged by a horse), and were adept in the use of sign language. Driven into Texas and up against

American Lutheran Church, Albert

Horse grazing, LBJ pasture

the Spanish frontier by Comanches, in company with Mescaleros, they were soon raiding Spanish settlements and missions at San Antonio and other frontier outposts. But so hard-pressed were they by the Comanches and other northern enemies, that they sought Spanish friendship in hopes of receiving assistance from them.

As a result, the San Saba mission and presidio were established for them in 1757, near present-day Menard. The mission was destroyed the following year by Comanches and their northern allies. The presidio held out a few years, but it, too, was ultimately abandoned.

In 1762, two missions were founded in the Upper Nueces Valley, San Lorenzo de la Santa Cruz and Nuestra Senora de la Candelaria, in what was thought to be safer territory. But the Comanches soon learned of these new missions, attacked them repeatedly, and they were abandoned in less than a decade. The Lipans continued to fight the Comanches when they were able to, raided the Spaniards and Mexicans whenever the prospects looked profitable, and generally sided with and fought for Texans and Americans in later years.

Comanches on the Warpath

The Comanches had also acquired horses sometime during the seventeenth century and had moved out into the plains

Gate to LBJ Ranch

of eastern Colorado and western Kansas from their mountain and plateau homeland. Without hesitation they attacked Spanish and Indian settlements in New Mexico and the Apaches on the plains. Before the eighteenth century was half over, the fury of their assault had gained them possession of much of the southern plains and had halted the advance of the Spanish frontier. They made repeated drives deep into areas occupied by the Lipans and raided the Central Texas frontier.

In early summer, when bison were fat, and in the fall, when the hides reached their prime, the Comanches embarked upon large-scale communal hunts. After locating a suitable herd, the hunting party approached from downwind and slowly encircled it, closing the gap on the upwind side last. The mounted hunters circled the herd and compressed it into as small an area as possible. If the herd could be made to mill about, its slaughter was that much easier.

When a herd could not be surrounded, a line of hunters might form downwind and charge the beasts at one time. Bison were also stampeded over cliffs, often with the aid of an agile boy who lured the animals on, disguised in a bison robe to which were attached horns and ears. The Comanches hunted other large game animals, and in South Texas where they were plentiful, hunted mustangs, whose flesh was highly regarded.

Skin shirts, buffalo robes, and hide overshoes equipped

LBJ Ranch entrance, over Pedernales

Comanches to withstand the coldest gales of the plains. In warm weather, men and boys went virtually naked; girls always wore some sort of clothing. Feathered war bonnets were adopted late in the nineteenth century, but they never attained the popularity they did in the northern plains.

Tipis were ideal homes for a nomadic people such as the Comanches. Women could erect them in a few moments and as rapidly dismantle them. Camps were usually located near running water and a large one might extend along a stream for several miles.

Born to be a Warrior

While children of both sexes were welcomed and loved, it was boys — the future warriors — who brought the greatest joy to a family. As soon as a boy had demonstrated his ability as a hunter and had acquired supernatural sanction, he was ready to take his place on a war party. His successful return signaled a dance of celebration and marked the beginning of adulthood. He was now eligible to marry, but he usually postponed this step until he had gained a reputation as a hunter and warrior. By so doing he was in a better position to acquire the wife of his choice. Normally, a man inherited his wife's younger sisters as additional wives, and he might take other women, especially captives, as wives also.

There were at one time about a dozen Comanche bands,

LBJ Ranch house and river

but there was no Comanche tribe in a political sense. Each band had a headman or chief who was not formally recognized or given a title, but who spoke with the authority of the consensus of the eminent men. Each band also recognized an eminent warrior as a paramount war chief.

Comanche culture came into being through military prowess and blossomed through raiding and brawling. Almost every aspect of life became intertwined in one way or another with war, and the reputation of Comanches as superb horsemen and courageous fighters is well deserved.

Comanche war parties struck swiftly, looted, killed, and as rapidly withdrew. When enemies could not be surprised, they might be ambushed, but only enemies very inferior in numbers and firepower were charged. Comanches were noted for their ability to withdraw more rapidly than any enemy could follow, but if hotly pursued, war parties quickly dispersed so that it was virtually impossible to engage them. It was not until the Texas Rangers adopted Colt's revolving pistol that the supremacy of the Comanches was challenged in the Hill Country and in the plains.

Meusebach's Treaty

Finally, in 1846, the Comanche hold on the Pedernales Valley was loosened. In May of that year, Baron von Meusebach led a wagon train of German settlers from New Braunfels to

First Family's swimming pool   *A President's Country*

establish Fredericksburg. Beyond the frontier and exposed to
Indian attack, the new settlement was in a precarious position
until the next spring, when Meusebach concluded a lasting
peace with the Comanches.

Actually, by this date there were few bison left in this
part of Texas, and the southern Comanches who ranged this
land had been considerably weakened by European diseases
and constant strife. In 1848, Fredericksburg was given added
protection by the construction of Fort Martin Scott, about
two miles from town on the old San Antonio-Fredericksburg
road. The frontier moved on west, however, and the Fort was
abandoned in 1866. The Pedernales Valley had become a
secure part of Texas and the United States.

Thus, the story of human experience in the Pedernales
Valley is one of successive waves of occupation, each flourish-
ing for a time, but ultimately giving way to other men following different stars, pursuing other ways of life.

WHERE THE DEER AND THE PAISANO PLAY

W. W. NEWCOMB, *Director*
and GERALD RAUN, *Curator of Zoology*
Texas Memorial Museum
The University of Texas

THERE IS NOTHING QUITE LIKE "A PRESIDENT'S COUNTRY" anywhere else in Texas.

Its location is in one of the seven distinct areas into which Texas has been divided according to the diversity and distribution of its plant and animal life. To biologists, it is known as the Balconian province, and it includes the major portion of the Edwards Plateau.

To Texans, it is the most distinct and unique of the state's biotic subdivisions. It is the only such subdivision that is truly Texan, because it is located entirely within the state. And it is the only biotic province which has species of wildlife found nowhere else.

It is the beginning of "the big sky country" of Texas. Here the east meets the west geographically, at the Balcones escarpment. Many species of plants and animals which are widely distributed in the eastern United States reach their western limits along the Balcones escarpment. On the Edwards Plateau, the flora and fauna become typically western in nature.

Scrub Forests of the Uplands

Here in the thin, rocky upland soils, are the evergreen scrub forests of Mexican cedar (*Juniperus ashei*) and Texas or Spanish oak (*Quercus texana*). In the fall, the landscape brightens with the flaming red of the sumac (*Rhus glabra, R. copallina*). And throughout the year, shrubs like the prickly

The late President's Herefords

pear (*Opuntia lindheimeri*) and sotol (*Dasylirium texanum*) contest with the native range grasses for water and life.

Sometimes the soil is so poor that the mixed scrub forests are dwarfed. Texans call these "shinnery." Uncleared areas of knee-high shinnery are often so dense that it is impossible to ride through them on horseback.

Contrasting with the shinnery are the almost impenetrable, pure stands of cedar. These are "cedar brakes" to the natives, and their abundance (this is the only timber of commercial importance) has given rise to a distinct socioeconomic group known as "cedar choppers."

Land of the Cedar Choppers

These isolated hill people, better known in myth and story than in fact, derive an often precarious existence from cutting and clearing the cedar brakes. Cedar is used mainly for fence posts, and there are several commercial cedar yards on the outskirts of Austin. Also along this highway the visitor may occasionally see the simple frame home of the cedar chopper.

Surprisingly, cedar brakes are more extensive today than they were in the days before ranchers allowed many parts of the Edwards Plateau to become overgrazed. Now the observant traveler will note that a determined effort is being made on a number of ranches to eradicate the cedar and thus improve the range.

Main house, LBJ Ranch

In the Valleys

The soils developed in the valleys on sandstones and on alluvial deposits support a varied growth of trees. These include post oak (*Quercus stellata*), usually found on sand or gravel terraces often in relatively pure stands, and along stream courses, pecans (*Carya illinoensis*), both the native and commercially improved strains, bald cypress (*Taxodium distichum*), cottonwood (*Populus deltoides*), and others.

Many trees characteristic of eastern forests have, in diminishing numbers, extended their ranges up the valleys into the Hill Country. Sycamores (*Platanus occidentalis*), American elms (*Ulmus americana*), cedar or cork elms (*Ulmus crassifolia*), and hackberries (*Celtis laevigata, C. occidentalis*) are a few of the more conspicuous. Grey-green crooked live oaks (*Quercus virginiana*), some growing for three centuries and to enormous size, are the most picturesque. Peach and plum trees have been introduced into the Pedernales Valley and the orchards are now numerous.

During the fall, the dark green of the evergreen cedar and the vivid reds and russets of the Spanish oaks, sumacs, and other deciduous trees and shrubs remind many people of the rolling, autumn hills of New England. If the traveler turns aside and follows the Sabinal River, an eastern tributary of the Frio River, the parallel will be even stronger, for scattered up and down the valley are the only sugar maples to be

President's office, LBJ Ranch   *President's hats, in Ranch den*

found in the Hill Country. Their brilliant fall colors provide a stark contrast to the nearby rocky cliffs.

Wildflowers and Shrubs

In spring, wildflowers transform the Hill Country and particularly the roadsides into a mass of color. Bluebonnets, the state's official flower, make many pastures seem a haze of blue; buttercups, phlox, verbenas, daisies, black-eyed-susans, firewheels, and dozens of other flowers carpet the countryside with a riot of color. While the height of the bloom is seen in early spring, many flowers continue to bloom into the long summer — the prickly poppies, ground-cherries, tompillos, nettles, sunflowers, and others.

Many of the shrubs of the Hill Country are also noted for their springtime flowers and aroma.

Probably the most spectacular is the Texas mountain laurel (*Sophora secundiflora*), a handsome evergreen shrub with small, lustrous green leaflets. Covered with clusters of lavender-blue flowers in early spring, so sweet and heavy is their scent that the hordes of butterflies and bees attracted to them seem drunk with delight.

Another shrub, known as agarita or simply chaparral (*Mahonia trifoliata*), is ordinarily inconspicuous with its sharp, tough, dull green leaves. But when in bloom, the small, pale yellow flowers have a clinging fragrance not soon forgotten.

48

View from President's window

The red berries ripen in May and make a fine preserve.

Wildlife is Plentiful

During the daylight hours the traveler is apt to see little of the wildlife of the Edwards Plateau, except possibly an occasional white-tailed deer (*Odocoileus virginianus*) or turkey (*Meleagaris gallopavo*). But at night the countryside comes to life, and the automobile driver must be cautious lest he collide with a deer, skunk, or 'possum.

Hunting is a major industry in this region and while thousands of deer are killed by hunters each year, over-population remains a serious problem in wildlife management. Probably at no time in the past has there been such an abundance of deer. One of the reasons for the over-abundance is that the larger predators have been almost eliminated, and even coyotes are relatively scarce.

Not too many years ago, mountain lions (*Felis concolor*), bobcats (*Lynx rufus*), ocelots (*Felis pardalis*), black bear (*Ursus americanus*), red wolves (*Canis niger*), coyotes (*Canis latrans*), and even an occasional jaguar (*Felis onca*) were present and in some instances, common. The gray wolf (*Canis lupus*) has long since disappeared. Bison, his chief prey, were early driven from the Plateau, and when the wolf shifted his attention to calves, sheep, and goats, stockmen waged a relentless campaign of extermination against him.

LBJ Ranch walk, with guests' signatures

Many of the smaller predators are still abundant and are glimpsed along the road at night.

The ring-tailed cat (*Bassariscus astutus*), which is not a cat at all but a member of the raccoon family, is one of these. Ring-tails are widely distributed over much of Texas but are probably most numerous in the limestone hills of the Edwards Plateau. Their relative, the raccoon (*Procyon lotor*), is also common on the Edwards Plateau and is apt to be seen at night.

Skunks are common and three different species may be seen: the striped skunk (*Mephitis mephitis*), the hog-nosed skunk (*Conepatus mesoleucas*), and the spotted skunk (*Spilogale putorius*). The opossum (*Didelphis marsupialis*) is another common nocturnal creature of the Plateau.

A number of other small mammals may be seen along the roads. In the wooded bottomlands, fox squirrels (*Sciurus niger*) scurry from branch to branch. Near cliffs, ledges, and other rocky situations, the rock squirrel (*Citellus variegatus*), about the size of a small house cat, is common. Both jackrabbits and cottontails are plentiful in parts of the Hill Country, as are many species of mice and rats.

The Little Armored Tank

One of the most interesting creatures to be seen in this region is the nine-banded armadillo (*Dasypus novemcinctus*),

an errant, bumbling, improbable mammal. Covered by a nine-banded "shell" with head and tail to match, it usually gives birth to four young which are always of the same sex. Once found only much farther south, this mammal has extended his range northward during the present century. Fond of ants and other insects, it prefers the soil and cover of valley floors.

Numerous caves are present in the limestones of the Plateau; some have been commercialized, but most are accessible only to experienced, well-equipped explorers. These caves commonly support huge populations of bats, predominantly of two species, the Mexican free-tailed bat (*Tadarida brasiliensis*) and the Mexican cave bat (*Myotis velifer*). One of the more spectacular caves, the Devil's Sinkhole in Edwards County, is estimated to house 8 million free-tailed bats along with smaller numbers of other species.

Salamanders and Snakes

The unique forms of wildlife on the Edwards Plateau are the salamanders, lizard-like creatures which live in or near water. One of the five salamanders (*Typholomolge rathbuni*) is known only from two caves and an artesian well in San Marcos, Hays County. Only one of the remaining four species has a general distribution in the streams and springs of the Plateau; the others are restricted to very limited areas, usually a single spring.

Wildflowers on LBJ Ranch

Poisonous snakes include the coral snake (*Micrurus fulvius*), commonly referred to as the most deadly snake in North America. This is untrue, since the coral snake is typically inoffensive and can seldom be induced to bite. Even when it does bite, the result is rarely fatal, for although its venom is quite toxic, it seldom can inject enough to kill a healthy adult.

The Texas diamond-back rattlesnake (*Crotalus atrox*) is dangerous, aggressive, and is probably responsible for more human deaths from snakebite than any other species in the United States. Other poisonous snakes found on the Edwards Plateau include the black-tailed rattlesnake (*Crotalus molossus*), copperhead (*Agkistrodon contortrix*), water moccasin (*Agkistrodon piscivorus*), and along the western edge an occasional rock rattlesnake (*Crotalus lepidus*).

These snakes are not as abundant as many Texas tales would have one believe, but it is always wise to walk carefully and to look before poking a hand into a bush or under a rock.

The vast majority of snakes are non-poisonous, non-aggressive, and despite the prejudices which people frequently harbor against them, are usually of economic benefit because they feed on destructive rodents and harmful insects. Non-poisonous snakes most frequently seen in this area include

Grave markers of President's parents

bull snakes, kingsnakes, coachwhips, whipsnakes, racers, garter snakes, and several varieties of water snakes.

The Texas long-nosed snake (*Rhinocheilus lecontei*), brightly colored and very attracive, is often mistaken for the coral snake. Actually, there is little resemblance except that the color pattern of both species is red, black, and yellow. The long-nosed snake has alternating red and black saddles, edged in yellow, while the coral snake has alternating rings of red, yellow, black, yellow, red.

Another harmless snake resembling the coral snake even more closely is the scarlet kingsnake (*Lampropeltis doliata*), which also has alternating rings of red, black, and yellow. The red and yellow rings of the coral snake connect, but the yellow of the kingsnake touches only its black rings.

Lizards, Swift and Slow

Many different kinds of lizards inhabit the Hill County, and their varied antics enthrall many people. The best known is the Texas horned lizard (often called "horned toad"). If molested he may squirt blood from his eyes! This bizarre habit presumably aids him to elude predators.

Probably the most abundant lizards are the rusty, or fence lizards (*Sceloporus undulatus, S. olivaceus*), but their coloration hides them from all but the sharp-eyed. Their favored habitats are trees, rocks, and fences. If a bright green streak

President's birthplace, Johnson City

darts from underfoot to disappear into the grass or leaves, it is probably the aptly-named racerunner (*Cnemidophorus gularis*). These beautiful lizards are often found around houses where they patrol flower beds and sidewalks in search of insects.

Another speedy lizard of the Plateau is the brilliantly colored and fearsome collared lizard or mountain boomer (*Crotaphytus collaris*). They inhabit rocky areas and with their over-sized heads and habit of running on the hind legs, resemble nothing so much as miniature carnivorous dinosaurs of the *Tyrannosaurus* type. Possessing strong jaws, a full-grown individual can bite hard enough to bring blood.

At the opposite end of the scale, as far as speed is concerned, is the Texas alligator lizard (*Gerrhonotus liocephalus*), a true slowpoke. Virtually limited to the Edwards Plateau, alligator lizards feed on insects and other small lizards which they stalk in slow motion among the limestone rocks. Where other lizards rely on speed, the alligator lizard relies on stealth, creeping slowly toward its prey until suddenly, in a bewildering reversal of form, it makes a short dash to pounce on its victim.

Birds that Fly — and Run

The Edwards Plateau is richly endowed with bird life, but the traveler will miss most species unless he abandons his

Stonewall's top attractions

car in favor of a stroll through the woods. Telephone and power lines, however, are favorite perches for shrikes or butcher birds, meadowlarks, swallows, scissor-tails, and the mockingbird, the state's official bird. An occasional red-tailed or red-shouldered hawk may stare balefully from a roadside tree but most often is seen wheeling in the blue sky overhead. Vultures, the most abundant of the large, scavenging birds, are grace personified in the air but are ungainly on the ground. They perform a valuable service as garbage collectors and highway cleaners, since they live primarily on carrion.

Turkeys, once common over much of the eastern United States, are abundant in many sections of the Edwards Plateau. A favorite of hunters, the traveler needs a sharp eye to spot this impressive bird. Dove and quail hunting are also popular in this land, and both the mourning dove and bobwhite quail are common along the roadsides.

The roadrunner or paisano is also a common bird on the Plateau and may occasionally be glimpsed from the highway, perhaps careening after a lizard or standing on a stump with a snake dangling from his beak. Like the late J. Frank Dobie, many Texans regard the paisano as more representative of the state than almost any other species of bird. Once you have encountered him along a highway, or watched him hurtle through the prickly pear, you will have been introduced properly to the broad country that was the President's homeland.

HOMES IN THE HILLS

DRURY B. ALEXANDER
School of Architecture
The University of Texas

MAC TATCHELL

JUST AS THE BALCONES ESCARPMENT GEOGRAPHICALLY DIVIDES the Old South from the West at Austin, so do the remaining examples of early architecture in the region show the division between two distinct cultures.

In Austin one finds the finest collection of Greek Revival mansions in Texas. Most prominent of these is the beautiful Governor's Mansion at 1010 Colorado, just south and west of the Capitol in downtown Austin. First occupied in 1855, the stately white brick structure with its six massive Ionic columns, hand-hewn from native Texas pine, was built at a cost of only $17,500. Designed in the classic Southern Plantation style, the Governor's Mansion, like the other old white columned homes of Austin, marks the final westward extension of the cotton culture of the Southern states.

(The Governor's Mansion is open to visitors Monday through Friday, from 10 a.m. to 12 noon.)

Southern Mansions and German Farmhouses

An equally beautiful example of Southern architecture is "Woodlawn," one of Texas' most historic private mansions, and today the home of former Governor and Mrs. Allan Shivers. Located at No. 6 Niles Road, in the exclusive Enfield district of Austin's west side, "Woodlawn" was purchased from its original owner by another Texas governor, E. M. Pease, and was first occupied in 1857. Like the Governor's

Sandy peach orchard, Stonewall

Mansion, "Woodlawn" is fronted by six huge white Ionic columns. Once the center of a 200-acre estate, the grounds today are among the largest of any private residence in Austin, occupying a square block. "Woodlawn" is closed to the public.

While the mansions of the Old South, as well as those of Victorian England and France, have left their influence on the architecture of Austin, this is less true of the area along Highway 290 west of Fredericksburg. Architecture in the city of Fredericksburg itself has little relation to the way of life on the Southern plantation. On the other hand, it is rich in examples of the 19th Century architecture which reveal the characteristics of the last significant national culture to enrich the heritage of 20th Century Texas — that of the German.

Log Cabins and Tin Storefronts

Between the Southern architecture of Austin and the German architecture of Fredericksburg are the log cabins, stone houses and barns, churches and even stores that reflect the influence of this rough and virile land on their builders. Here, too, one can sense the merging of the two cultures — that of the Old South with the New West.

A log cabin, for example, will suggest that the builder was from a Southern state or from East Texas where such structures were typical of the westward-moving frontier. The stone houses are almost invariably the work of German

Picking famed Stonewall peaches

colonists who arrived in this part of Texas in the late 1840's, bringing with them their traditional skill as masons.

Roofs tell much about the origin of the builder. If the house has a steeply pitched and gabled roof, it almost certainly was built by a German following the medieval traditions of his homeland. A low-pitched roof, with a slight break where the porch joins the house, indicates a builder influenced by the architecture of the Southern states. Deep porches running across the front of the house are characteristic of Southern architecture.

En route from Austin through "a President's country," the traveler along Highway 290 passes a two-story frame and stone store at Oak Hill which is typical of the old general merchandise emporium so necessary to this area at the turn of the century. The old store, built in 1898 by J. H. Patton, still welcomes the wayfarer today, as the Fortress Restaurant.

Twenty-two miles west of Austin, at Dripping Springs, the visitor finds a community whose architecture still bears a trace of the Old West. Highway 290 misses the principal business district, but a turn north for a block or so brings the visitor to a Main Street lined with stone buildings that are reminiscent of a set for a television or movie western.

On the south side of the old highway between Dripping Springs and Johnson City is a remodeled and enlarged log cabin which is still serving as a home. The small windows on

19th century house, Stonewall

either side of the chimney indicate that it is an early example.

A short distance west, on the north side of the highway, is a small stone structure which apparently was built as a home. This building, handsomely located on a rise of land overlooking a rocky terrace of Miller Creek, has the earmarks of a German house: a steeply pitched roof, well-fitted blocks of cut stone in the walls and chimney, and two small windows in the gable and on either side of the chimney. These windows gave light to the loft area which served as sleeping quarters for the family.

Johnson City has a number of interesting stone buildings including the Blanco County Courthouse in the center of the town square and a sturdy stone jail house facing it on the southeast corner (visiting hours posted by the door). At the southwest edge of Johnson City is a cluster of stone barns and farm buildings constructed in the 1850's by the President's grandfather, Sam Ealy Johnson, and his brother, Tom, which provide good examples of the quality of masonry work found in this area. One of these, a small square building with a pyramidal roof, must have been a smokehouse where early settlers cured their meats by slowly smoking them.

At Hye, there is a combined post office and general store in a building which was erected in 1902. Especially interesting is its pressed tin front. The elaborate design has at some

Victorian frame farmhouse, Stonewall

time been picked out with red, white, and green paint, giving it a startlingly gay effect.

Between Stonewall and Fredericksburg are two Victorian farmhouses. On the south side of the highway is a large two-story stone house with a gallery across the front, and on the north side of the highway is a white frame house.

On Ranch Road 1

Just west of Hye, beyond the Blanco-Gillespie County line, Ranch Road 1 intersects with Highway 290. This is the 4.6 miles that takes the visitor by the LBJ Ranch and also alongside some of the many historic buildings in the area.

At the point where Ranch Road 1 turns west, the American Lutheran Church of Albert, faced with pressed tin, stands. Pressed tin was one of the favorite building materials of the early German settlers and this is one of the finest remaining examples of this kind of construction.

Less than a mile down the road, on the north bank of the Pedernales River, stands the LBJ Ranch house. The architecture is pure Texan — a style that combines a little of the Old South with the variations made necessary by the land.

Just 2.4 miles west of the LBJ Ranch is the St. Francis Xavier Catholic Church, another example of the early church architecture in "a President's country." And just beyond the church is an old-style stone house built of Comanche Peak

Victorian stone farmhouse, Stonewall

Limestone which is one of the best-preserved examples of a German settler's home.

Proceeding onto the western intersection of Ranch Road 1 and Highway 290, the traveler passes through Stonewall, the community that claims President Johnson as its native son. Some 13 miles farther west, the visitor enters Fredericksburg, one of the most interesting communities in Texas from an architectural standpoint.

Fascinating Fredericksburg

Fredericksburg has a fascinating collection of early Texas German architecture that is remarkably well preserved. The examples range from the small half timber and stone houses and large stone churches of the first decades of the settlement to the later Victorian residential and commercial architecture of the 1880's and '90's.

On Main Street in Fredericksburg is the Kammlah House, now the Pioneer Museum, constructed of *fachwerk* or half timber construction. This type of building in which the timber frame is exposed on the exterior and interior, reveals a tradition that goes back to medieval Europe. Also on Main Street are many early stone houses and stores as well as others of a later period. Notable is the elaboration of detail so common in the 1880's and 1890's and the cast iron store fronts. The

Cross Mountain, Fredericksburg

handsome stone detail on the Richardsonian Romanesque Bank alone is worth a close inspection by anyone interested in architecture.

Of special interest in Fredericksburg is the *Vereins Kirche*, or Coffeemill Church, which is a modern replica of the original built in 1846. It now serves as the Chamber of Commerce. This hexagonal-shaped building was a unique form of church architecture.

Unique Sunday Houses

The church was second only to the home of the early German settlers and to miss a Sunday meeting at the *kirche* was rare. However, attending services frequently meant a long slow wagon trip to town and back. To provide a place to rest and relax between these comings and goings, many German farmers built structures that are unique in Texas — the Sunday house.

A few of these Sunday houses still stand in Fredericksburg today. They are easily recognized by their diminutive size, their story-and-a-half form and the outside stairs which lead up to the attic bedroom. Most of them also have a front porch, and behind the roof of the porch, the house is raised slightly to provide space in the attic for sleeping quarters.

Because Saturday was a traditional trade day, farmers often drove into town with their families to do their week's

Old Nimitz Hotel, Fredericksburg

shopping, spent the night in their Sunday house and then returned home after services.

The Nimitz Hotel

Visitors have long been intrigued by the famous old Nimitz Hotel, a landmark on Fredericksburg's main street. It was the best-known stopping-place on the long and dusty military road from the western frontier to San Antonio. The first building, erected in 1847 by Charles H. Nimitz, was replaced in 1855 by a rambling two-story lumber and adobe structure which included a casino, ballroom-theater, saloon, brewery and general store, as well as hotel accommodations.

This center for entertainment and rest, with its narrow superstructure at front, resembling the upper deck of a river steamer, attracted visitors of note. Its old registers show the stagecoaches brought to the Nimitz such figures as R. E. Lee, Rutherford B. Hayes, Phil Sheridan and a quiet gentleman who always signed as "C. S. Howard, El Paso," but was better known as Jesse James.

And from the Nimitz Hotel came a clear-eyed square-jawed young man, grandson of the original Charles H. Nimitz, whose name would be known world-wide. He was to be Admiral Chester Nimitz of the United States Navy.

Present Nimitz Hotel, Fredericksburg

Saint Barnabas' Mission

Even today, Fredericksburg is a city of churches, and old St. Mary's Catholic Church long has been a favorite of tourists. Perhaps the most visited church in the city today, however, is the tiny St. Barnabas Episcopal Mission.

Although the St. Barnabas Mission was formed only in 1952, it is housed in a building that dates back to 1848. The ceiling still has its hand-made caliche and straw around cypress boards. All of the furniture in the church, except the organ, is hand-made.

It is here on a Sunday that President and Mrs. Johnson usually came to worship when they were in residence at the LBJ Ranch.

THE EVERLASTING LAND

PETER T. FLAWN
*President, The University of Texas
at San Antonio*

"A PRESIDENT'S COUNTRY" IS WHERE THE WEST REALLY BEGINS.

The landscape of Texas changes abruptly and dramatically at Austin. A traveler coming from the East and crossing the Texas Gulf Coastal Plain finds that the rolling prairie ends suddenly at the Capital City, where a line of wooded hills rises as much as 300 feet above the undulating plain.

Geologists know this change in the landscape as the Balcones escarpment, and yet it isn't really an escarpment. Millions of years ago, the earth's crust in the area broke — the Hill Country went up and the Coastal Plain went down. Today the fracture, or fault, is marked by a line of hills, indented by a number of valleys, which is, in the opinion of many, the most beautiful part of Texas.

The Line Between South and West

These hills, however, are more than the mere surface expression of a major fracture of the land. This great break in the earth's crust is also the visible line that separates the Old South from the West. In a very real sense, it is a sort of "divide" which splits the culture and economy of Texas into two very distinct and separate halves.

Thus, when President Johnson called himself a "westerner," he was geographically correct. Sixty miles to the east of his birthplace, on the eastern side of the Balcones escarpment, are the rich blacklands where cotton and grain sorghums

Bust of Baron Meuseback   *Old Bank of Fredericksburg*

flourish and farming is the way of life. To the west of Austin, however, in the country where the President was born and died, the land is rugged and western — ranch country.

Here the blacklands disappear and the soil is thin and rocky. Farming still goes on, but only the thicker soils of the valleys are cultivated. For the most part, the land is given over to cattle, sheep and goat ranches.

Tending herds is one of man's oldest occupations, and it may be symbolic that ranching is still the principal way of life in the Texas Hill Country. It is an old land, geologically speaking, and a land to which change has come slowly.

An Old Sea Floor

The Cretaceous limestones and clays that form the steep, rocky ledges are estimated by geologists to be about 100 to 120 million years old. Originally this was the bottom of a great sea, and many of the rocks found in the area contain evidences of ocean life. Rock hunters frequently find fossil oysters, clams, large snails and sea urchins. Fossil hunting is a popular pastime in the Edwards Pleateau.

Along the valley of the Pedernales River, which fronts the LBJ Ranch, the land is even older. Some of the rocks in the valley are Precambrian — 1,000 to 1,100 million years old. They crop out as granite knobs which have been partly

68

German Sunday house, Fredericksburg

exhumed from the sediments that have buried them.

Two fine examples of these primeval rocks can be seen easily by visitors to "a President's country." One small knob is north of the Pedernales just about opposite the little community of Hye. A more spectacular one is Bear Mountain, 4 miles north of Fredericksburg on Farm Road 965.

It has been said of the Texas Hill country that it produces nothing but "cows, cedar and rock." To a degree, this is true, because the area does produce fine cattle, it has thousands of acres of cedar trees and its formations of limestone are as commanding as can be found anywhere in the country. During the great drought of the middle 50's, a hard-bitten rancher gazed across his scarred pasture at the heat reflecting off the limestone hills and was heard to remark, "If only that limestone rock was worth ten cents a pound."

The rocks of the hill country are mostly hard limestone and cherty (or flint-bearing) limestone, softer clayey limestone or marl, and limy clay. Where they have been cut by streams (and the area abounds with spring-fed streams), their layered structure is plainly visible. The hard layers form the steep, rocky ledges with their thin soils, which are so common in this area. The soft layers form relatively flat benches and here the soils are deeper and locally are cultivated.

Chamber of Commerce, once Vereins Kirche, Fredericksburg

Peaches from the Sands

Not all of this rough and hardy land is given over to limestone and clay, however. On the low slopes of the hills, and in parts of the Pedernales River Valley, there is a sequence of sand, silt, clay and conglomerate known to geologists as the Hensell Sand. This sand is of Cretaceous age and was deposited when this part of Texas was a warm, shallow sea. Today it provides the soil for the famous peach orchards which grow in the sandy loam around Stonewall and Fredericksburg.

Stonewall, in fact, is so proud of its peaches that signs along Highway 290 on the outskirts of town long have given equal billing to its two claims to fame. They proclaim it: "The Home of LBJ — and the Peach Capital of the World."

Just as the rocks and soil have made peach-growing centers of Stonewall and Fredericksburg, they also have caused subtle changes in the growth and character of Austin, largest of the cities in "a President's country."

The Many Faces of Austin

Austin is built on rocks on the other side of the Balcones fault system from the Hill Country. Known as Upper Cretaceous rocks and having an age of 80 to 100 million years, they include limestone, chalk, marl and clay younger than those in the Pedernales Valley. Each has a characteristic

Three construction types: log, fachwerk, masonry — Fredericksburg

topography and distinguishing vegetation with the result that the city of Austin changes subtly as the soil changes.

The chalk, for example, supports the larger structures in the city — the downtown business area, the State Capitol buildings and the campus of The University of Texas. The chalk forms a rolling, hilly landscape with open grasslands and "mottes" of live oak trees. It creates a landscape reminiscent of the famed English downs.

Austin begins to lose its kinship with the English countryside at its eastern outskirts. Here the chalk belt ends and the so-called Taylor prairie begins. This is a part of the famous blackland belt, or black prairie, of central Texas. The heavy black clay soils crack deeply in hot, dry weather and become tenaciously adhesive when wet, but they are some of the richest farmland in the nation. Perhaps this is why this suburban area sometimes reminds visitors of the fine croplands of Illinois and the Middle West.

If Austin is geographically English at its center and Middle Western on its eastern edges, it is pure American West on its opposite extremity. Between the downtown section and the beginning of the real Hill Country, the face of the land changes again — this time to belts of alternating limestone and clay. Outcrops of Edwards and Georgetown limestone appear and the rich soil disappears.

Old-timers used to call the uninhabited area between the

St. Barnabas Episcopal Church, Fredericksburg

western hills and the Missouri Pacific Railroad "hard scrabble," or Bear Creek country. Now that these near hills have become the city's largest and most desirable residential area, home owners still regard it somewhat as "hard scrabble" because they have to haul in topsoil before lawns will grow. Hackberry and mesquite trees grow well in the clay, but almost everything else requires better soil.

Most Beautiful in Texas

Austin residents recognize their city's varied topography as a problem, but most of them wouldn't want to live anywhere else. The city that was a second home of President Johnson has been called the most beautiful in Texas and this is probably not an overstatement.

When President Mirabeau B. Lamar of the Republic of Texas appointed a commission to select a site for the future capital, he charged them to find the most beautiful spot in the Republic. In 1839, they selected the point where the Colorado River emerges from the Hill Country as the most scenic in all of Texas.

A City of Seven Terraces

Like ancient Rome, modern Austin is built on seven hills, or terraces, formed by the river. It was at least a million years ago when the first of the great ice masses moved south-

St. Barnabas Church sign, Fredericksburg   St. Barnabas Church interior

ward over North America and changed the climate. Like other rivers, the Colorado responded to the high volume of water entering its watershed and began a vigorous erosion of the land, cutting down through the rocks and leaving a record of its higher courses in a series of terraces. At Austin, the valley of the Colorado is six miles wide and its terraces have become so populated with buildings that they are difficult to trace.

The visitor, however, can find the most prominent of the seven by locating the landmarks built upon them. Highest of the terraces is still known around town as the Asylum because the state hospital for the mentally ill is built on its 600-foot elevation in north Austin. Still following the line of this highest terrace, but located about two miles to the east, is the Municipal Airport.

Texas' huge red granite Capitol, second only to the Capitol in Washington in size, dominates the second terrace. The Capitol terrace has an elevation from 540 to 560 feet and its base is 120 feet above the river, only 11 blocks down Congress Avenue.

Austin's third recognizable terrace is along Sixth Street and is about ten feet lower than the Capitol terrace. Sixth street follows this shelf west until it becomes Lake Austin Boulevard, one of the beautiful scenic drives into the residential areas in the hills.

Bear Mountain's granite blocks, Fredericksburg

Below Sixth Street, most of the downtown business section is built on a fourth terrace, which ranges from an elevation of 520 feet on the west to 450 feet on the east. The lowest of the seven terraces is on the south bank of the Colorado and is easily recognizable because it is the site of the Municipal Auditorium. It is here on the Auditorium grounds that the President's helicopter usually landed or took off when he travelled between Austin and the LBJ Ranch. Less well developed surfaces occur between the two prominent low terraces.

Because Austin is built on a series of terraces, some of its streets and avenues, particularly in the downtown area, have steep inclines rare in Texas cities. These have prompted some visitors to compare Austin with San Francisco, although the streets in the California city are much steeper and there are many more inclines.

A Slowly Changing Land

Just as Austin's terraces have been eroded slowly by both nature and man, all of "a President's country" is changing. The change, however, comes slowly and it is unlikely that it will be speeded up by any cataclysm of nature.

Unlike many of the great fault systems in California and Alaska, on the mobile and restless western margin of the continent, the Balcones fault is not active. In other words, "a President's country" is not likely to be disturbed by

Leaving a President's Country

earthquake. Although a minor earthquake attributed to movement along a fault was recorded in northeast Texas and southeast Oklahoma in 1934, there are no documented reports of major earth movements in central Texas in recorded history. In fact, there is no geological evidence to indicate that these faults, or fractures, have moved or changed much in recent geologic time, or that large-scale movement will occur in the future.

"A President's country" is an old and stable land which has withstood well the vicissitudes of time. It is likely to be very much the same a hundred or a thousand years in the future — a cradle for independent and self-reliant Americans.

The Lyndon Baines Johnson Library and Sid Richardson Hall

EPILOGUE

HARRY J. MIDDLETON
Director, Lyndon Baines Johnson Library
Austin, Texas

Lyndon Johnson gave the land in this book the inevitable stamp "A President's Country". Observers who watched the driving force of the leader who sought to complete a social revolution with an avalanche of legislation looked for the wellsprings of his passion, his concern and his energy. Invariably their search led them to the region chronicled in these chapters, its character and the traditions of its people. When he died, there were many eulogies, but none truer than the simple one voiced by the Congressman who occupied the seat Johnson had once held: "[He] came from the land, from the Hill Country of Texas, where sun and rain are the most precious values a man can tie to; and where God's will is seen and felt and gauged by the sky and the wind. It was from this land that Lyndon Johnson drew his strength." Those who traveled with him from the White House to the Ranch would observe with amazement how he would leap from the plane when it touched down at the air strip, get into a car with Mrs. Johnson, drive along the roads and across the fields of the Ranch, and return to the house a renewed man.

During those same years of power and responsibility, he proudly demonstrated his deep affection for the land and its resources. Presidents, chancellors and prime ministers dined in the ranch house where his plain and sturdy forebears had gathered for family festivities; they were treated to the sectional epicurean pleasures of barbecue and pinto beans. They were entertained by high school choirs and country

77

The LBJ family at the ranch

singers and dancers. The places of interest they were taken to see were the Coliseums, the Etoiles and the Versailles of the Hill Country—the German houses of Fredericksburg, the forts at Johnson City, and always the pastures where deer leaped at dusk and where the land in the day's last glimmering light projected an endless promise of serenity. Aides were summoned from their offices in Washington to chairs under a giant live oak on the Pedernales to hammer out the progrms that would combat poverty, advance education, and certify the civil rights of the oppressed.

Through it all there was a democracy in this Texas White House not often seen in the councils of the great. Seated around the table in the ranch house dining room during those vivid years might be several cabinet officers, the ranch foreman, the minister of the Lutheran Church across the road whose sermons were spiced with startling visual effects in which the President delighted, and an elderly presidential cousin whose deafness would present considerable complications to a presidential lunch-time discourse.

After he left the White House, the President who had taken his pleasure and his solace from the land, put into it the devotion and hard work he had previously invested in programs of national scope and significance. Those who wondered where his restless drive would take him watched him, quite simply, become a rancher.

He had four years. They were marred by failing health, but

Lyndon Baines Johnson State Park

they were busy years. He wrote his memoirs—his own account of the major events of his presiency. He watched, with care and interest, the birth of a School of Public Affairs, to train young men and women for public service, and the construction of the great library which bears his name, on the campus of The University of Texas at Austin. When the library was completed he deposited there the papers and memorabilia he had amassed in the course of four decades of public life, for scholars and visitors alike who would encounter a passage in their nation's history—and a piece of their own lives.

But above all, it was the land which consumed his interest. He converted his ranch into a green oasis in those hills of rock and cactus. And before his time was up, he saw to it that the ranch which bears his brand, and where history turned for a while, would be given to the American people, as a place where generations can come, and reflect, and from that reflection, perhaps learn—but in any event, enjoy.

Visitors can also take advantage of the pleasures of the LBJ State Park—across Ranch Road 1 from the ranch itself—270 acres where buffalo graze and where the traditions and artifacts of an earlier Texas are carefully preserved, recalling the Comanches who roamed the hills, and the German immigrants who came to homestead, and the cowboys who drove their cattle to the old Chisholm Trail. Because of the interest Johnson took in this historic and recreational facility,

LBJ's grave in the Johnson family cemetery

Park visitors will also be able to picnic, and relax, and walk along memorable scenic trails.

And many will stop for a moment at the gravesite of the thirty-sixth President of the United States. For he is buried where he chose to be, in the family cemetery beside the Pedernales, on the land that his ancestors cultivated.

When Carl Sandburg died in 1967, President Lyndon Johnson said of him: "He is part of the earth that he celebrated . . . . He is part of the American earth."

With a slight variation, it can be said as well of LBJ: He is part of the American earth, that special part of earth that will be known forever as A President's Country, which shaped his life and his dreams, and consequently a substantial part of the American saga.

ROAD LOG : AUSTIN TO FREDERICKSBURG

0.0	Intersection of Barton Springs Road and Bouldin Ave. Southwest corner of Municipal Auditorium. Looking north across Colorado River to site of first settlement in Austin.	*76.5*
0.3	Intersection of Barton Springs Road and South Lamar Blvd. (U. S. Highway 290). Turn left (south) on Lamar Blvd.	*76.2*
3.4	Intersection of South Lamar Blvd. and Ben White Blvd.	*76.1*
3.5	View to west of Edwards Plateau and drainage of Colorado River. The valley near the highway is that of Barton Creek which heads in the Hill Country west of Austin and north of U.S. Highway 290 and joins the Colorado at Zilker Park in southwest Austin. Vegetation consists of thick growths of cedar (juniper), live-oak, and mesquite.	*73.0*
5.0	This is the area where cedar is cleared for commercial use. Here and there along the highway an occasional "cedar chopper's" cabin may be seen.	*71.5*
7.2	Oak Hill community. On north side of road is a two-story stone store built in 1898.	*69.3*
8.1	Intersection of U.S. Highway 290 and State Highway 71. Turn west (left) on U.S. Highway 290. State Highway 71 is a favorite route to the Highland Lakes area of Central Texas.	*68.4*
9.1	Farm Road 1826 (south) to Camp Ben McCulloch. Camp Ben McCulloch was organized in 1896 as a reunion camp for Confederate veterans. Annual 3-day reunions were held until 1946. Ben McCulloch was a hero of the Texas Republic, an organizer of the Texas Rangers, a representative in the first Texas State Legislature, and a Confederate brigadier-general. He was killed in 1862 at the battle of Elk Horn, Arkansas.	*67.4*
14.5	Travis-Hays County line.	*62.0*
21.8	Dripping Springs. Many old stone buildings line Main Street, one block north of U.S. Highway 290. Ranch Road 12, which intersects Highway 290 here, leads to Wimberley, 13 miles south, famous for its dude ranches.	*54.7*
24.7	Roadside park on south side of highway.	*51.8*
26.9	View of valley of Onion Creek to south. This is one of the Hill Country's prettiest streams.	*49.6*
28.9	Earth-dammed stock tank south of highway. These	*47.6*

Mileage from Austin		Mileage from Fredericksburg
	are common in the Hill Country and are vital as a water supply for cattle.	
29.7	Henly community.	46.8
30.0	Farm Road 165 south to Blanco.	46.5
30.4	Peach orchard on soft clay layer in the Glen Rose Limestone. Orchards in the Glen Rose are rare; the older established peach orchards in the Stonewall-Fredericksburg area are in soils developed on the Hensell Sand, which underlies the Glen Rose Limestone.	46.1
30.8	View of Pedernales River valley to north.	45.7
31.1	A. Robinson Road (to Honeycut Bend)	45.4
31.2	Note stair-step topography in Glen Rose south of road.	45.3
31.3	Hays-Blanco County line.	45.2
32.5	Clear spots on surrounding hills are areas where cedar trees have been removed as part of a range improvement program.	44.0
34.6	Yeager Creek. (No road sign.)	41.9
36.1	Middle Creek. (No road sign.)	40.4
36.1	West end of U.S. Highway 290	40.4
40.5	Intersection of U.S. Highways 290 and 281. Turn north (right) on U.S. Highway 290.	36.0
		35.9
40.6	Miller Creek crossing.	35.6
40.9	Roadside park on west side of highway.	
45.9	Note house with broken-pitch roof on south side of road. This "Southern States" style house is typical of the area.	30.6
46.0	Intersection of U.S. Highways 290 and 281. Turn west (left) on U.S. Highway 290 to Fredericksburg.	30.5
46.4	The Blanco County Courthouse and jail, one block north of Highway 290, are typical of early construction in this part of Texas.	30.1
46.8	Cluster of three old stone farm buildings south of highway. These are among the best examples of early construction by German artisans.	29.7
47.1	Johnson City city limits. This is the community that was "home" to President Johnson. Here the visitor may see the house in which he grew up, the high school from which he was graduated and meet residents who have known the President since boyhood.	29.4
47.7	Flat Creek. Alluvium and Hensell Sand. Pecan trees on Hensell Sand.	28.8
50.7	Towhead Creek.	25.8
52.8	German-style stone house on south side of road.	23.7

53.4	Peach orchards.	23.1
53.8	Rocky Creek and Rocky Creek community. Rock cropping out in creek bottom is dolomite of Cambrian age and is the oldest sedimentary rock in the area.	22.7
55.0	Farm Road 1120 north to Brady.	21.5
56.0	Roadside park on north side of highway.	20.5
56.4	Hye community. Note old cotton gin on north side of road. Changes in agricultural economics forced cotton out of this area by the early 1930's. Combined post office and general store with pressed tin front was built in the early 1900's.	20.1
56.8	Road follows Pedernales River.	19.7
57.5	Blanco-Gillespie County Line.	19.0
58.6	Ranch Road 1 (Pedernales River loop) to north. Take this road to L.B.J. Ranch.	17.9

Log of Ranch Road 1:

0.0   East intersection of Ranch Road 1 and U.S. Highway 290. Turn north on Ranch Road 1.

0.2   Road turns west. On the left side of the road is the American Lutheran Church of Albert, which has a pressed tin facing and

road is the American Lutheran Church of Albert, which has a pressed tin facing and is one of the few remaining buildings of this construction. Road follows south bank of Pedernales River.

1.0   Entrance to the L.B.J. Ranch, home of the President and Mrs. Johnson.

3.4   St. Francis Xavier (Catholic) Church on south side of road.

3.6   Old-style stone house on south side of road represents pioneer architecture in the German-settled parts of central Texas. The stone is Comanche Peak Limestone.

4.6   West intersection of Ranch Road 1 with U.S. Highway 290.

Return to main road log at east intersection of U.S. Highway 290 and Ranch Road 1.

61.4	Farm Road 1623 south to Albert. In this area, north of U.S. Highway 290, is the LBJ State Park which welcomes visitors. The park includes a herd of Texas Longhorn cattle, picnic facilities, etc.	15.1
61.5	Entering Stonewall, the community that advertises that it's the "peach capital of the world." The center ofpeace-growing in the area, Stonewall also claimed President Johnson as a citizen because of	15.0

the town's proximity to the LBJ Ranch.

Mileage from Austin		Mileage from Fredericksburg
62.7	Intersection of U.S. Highway 290, and west end of Ranch Road 1.	13.8
63.5	Mexican cemetery, Cementerio Nuestra Senora de Guadalupe, on south side of highway.	13.0
65.2	Victorian farmhouse on south side of U.S. Highway 290 is built of Comanche Peak Limestone. Note typical post-oak vegetation on Hensell Sand and live-oak on gravel and limestone.	11.3
66.3	Roadside park on north side of highway.	10.2
66.4	South Grape Creek.	10.1
67.2	Blumenthal community.	9.3
70.3	Hills in the distance on north and south sides of U.S. Highway 290 at this point are part of the high surface of the Edwards Plateau.	6.2
71.1	Road to Cain City on south side of highway.	5.4
71.3	Roadside park on north side of highway.	3.7
71.7	Pedernales River crossing.	4.8
71.3	Roadside park to south.	3.7
73.7	Barons Creek crossing.	2.8
73.9	Fredericksburg city limit. Note numerous German-style buildings in Fredericksburg.	2.6
74.1	Historic marker on north side of highway is the site of Fort Martin Scott, established in 1848 and abandoned in 1866.	2.4
76.1	Junction of U.S. Highways 290 and 87. Historic Nimitz Hotel on north corner.	0.4

The original Nimitz Hotel, a one-story structure, was built in 1847 by Charles H. Nimitz, a German seaman who settled in Fredericksburg in 6. In 1855 Nimitz built a two-story adobe and lumber hotel which housed a casino, ballroom, stage, saloon, brewery, and general store. The Nimitz Hotel was a community center and a favorite of tourists. Some time later a narrow superstructure resembling the upper deck of a ship was added. The hotel was maintained for 61 years by the elder Nimitz and continued by his son, Charles, Jr., until the building was razed and the present structure erected on the same site in 1926. After 116 years of operation, the hotel now serves as a museum.

| 76.5 | Gillespie County courthouse. | 0.0 |

END OF ROAD LOG

Road Guide

to

A PRESIDENT'S COUNTRY

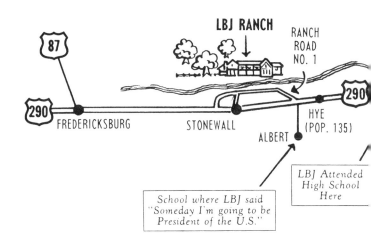

LBJ RANCH

RANCH ROAD NO. 1

87

290

FREDERICKSBURG

STONEWALL

ALBERT

HYE (POP. 135)

290

LBJ Attended High School Here

School where LBJ said "Someday I'm going to be President of the U.S."